RIO DE JANEIRO

THE CITY AT A GLANCE

CW00410313

Catédral Metropolitano
Big, black, brutal, but undeniabl...
Rio's massive modern cathedra...
in 1976, can hold a congregatio...
See p077

Santos Dumont Airport
Nobody could claim that Rio's domestic
airport isn't convenient. Flights in and
out offer stunning views over the city.

Museu de Arte Contemporânea
Oscar Niemeyer's 'flying saucer' in Niterói
has proved a late-career crowd-pleaser.
See p065

Parque do Flamengo
Roberto Burle Marx was landscape architect
by appointment to modern Rio. The Parque
do Flamengo is cleverly landscaped landfill,
stretching from the airport to Botafogo Bay.

Urca
An oasis of sleepy, shaded streets and lovely
early 20th-century architecture, best known
as the neighbourhood beneath Sugar Loaf.

Sugar Loaf
The second most famous mountain in the
world, and one of a series of impossibly
lush, soft-edge mounds that surround Rio.
See p010

Leme
A mile-long strip of beach at the north end
of Copacabana, popular with families, favela
boys (generally well-behaved) and fishermen.

Copacabana Beach
The most famous beach in the world is a bit
of a dump. But it's also 8km of stunning white
sand and fascinating beach life.

INTRODUCTION
THE CHANGING FACE OF THE URBAN SCENE

Let's face it, in recent years there has been something of the tired old tart about Rio, a city that might serve Testino well: stocked full of tanned, lithe lovelies, but with little to offer of substance. While both São Paolo and Buenos Aires come off as dynamic, ambitious and bursting with creative energy, as well as more aggressively urban, Rio dedicates itself to denying the urban; it's a city wedged between beaches and mountains after all. Then again, only the perverse would not make use of these natural advantages. What you get is a city low on cut-and-thrust, but big on the swinging and sensual. And Rio sure does swing.

But this is also a city that's constantly looking to improve itself, which makes for an architectural patchwork of old colonial and its trademark curvaceous modernism. While there may be no plans to rip up, pick up and landfill on a grand scale (as happened between the 1930s and 1960s), and the proposed Rio Guggenheim scheme has floundered, this is still a shifting city, fluid and flighty.

Leblon, ever tony, gets tonier, with Rua Dias Ferreira emerging as the new restaurant and retail hot-spot, and each new arrival pushing to look sharper and sleeker than the last. Lapa's old crumbling colonial mansions have been turned into swaying samba venues or antique and mid-century furniture stores. Sometimes both at the same time. It's gentrification as only Rio could do it and, for the moment, it's a whole heap of fun.

ESSENTIAL INFO
FACTS, FIGURES AND USEFUL ADDRESSES

TOURIST OFFICE
Avenida Princesa Isabel 183
T 2541 7522
www.riodejaneiro-turismo.com.br

TRANSPORT
Car hire
Avis
T 3398 5060
Hertz
T 3398 4338
Metro
T 0800 595 1111
Helicopter
T 2511 2141
www.helisight.com.br
Taxis
Central de Táxi
T 2593 2598
Coopertramo Radiotaxi
T 2560 2022

EMERGENCY SERVICES
Ambulance
T 192
Police
T 190
Tourist Police
T 3399 7170
24-hour pharmacy
Avenida Prado Junior 237a
T 3323 9000

CONSULATES
British Consulate-General
Praia do Flamengo 284
T 2555 9600
www.fco.gov.uk
US Consulate-General
Avenida Presidente Wilson 147
T 3823 2000
www.embaixadaamericana.org.br

MONEY
American Express
Copacabana Palace, Avenida Atlântica 1702
T 0800 702 0777

POSTAL SERVICES
Post Office
Avenida N S de Copacabana 540a
T 2256 1448
Shipping
UPS
T 0800 109226
www.ups.com

BOOKS
The Silence of the Rain by
Luiz Alfredo Garcia-Roza (Picador)
Rio de Janeiro: Carnival Under Fire
by Ruy Castro (Bloomsbury)
Futebol: The Brazilian Way of Life
by Alex Bellos (Bloomsbury)

WEBSITES
Art and architecture
www.vitruvius.com.br
www.mamrio.com.br
Newspapers
www.jb.com.br
www.jornaldocommercio.com.br

COST OF LIVING
**Taxi from Santos Dumont Airport
to Centro**
€16
Cappuccino
€0.40
Packet of cigarettes
€0.45
Daily newspaper
€0.70
Bottle of champagne
€39

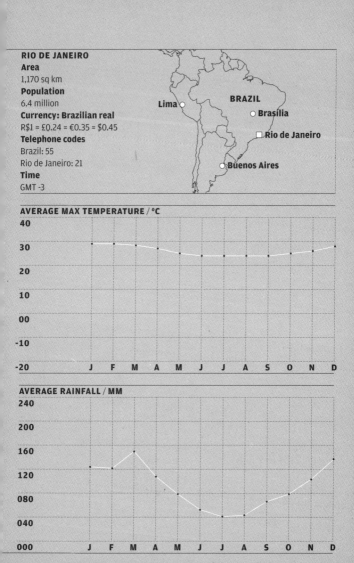

RIO DE JANEIRO
Area
1,170 sq km
Population
6.4 million
Currency: Brazilian real
R$1 = £0.24 = €0.35 = $0.45
Telephone codes
Brazil: 55
Rio de Janeiro: 21
Time
GMT -3

Lima
BRAZIL
Brasília
Rio de Janeiro
Buenos Aires

AVERAGE MAX TEMPERATURE / °C

40
30
20
10
00
-10
-20
        J   F   M   A   M   J   J   A   S   O   N   D

AVERAGE RAINFALL / MM

240
200
160
120
080
040
000
        J   F   M   A   M   J   J   A   S   O   N   D

NEIGHBOURHOODS

THE AREAS YOU NEED TO KNOW AND WHY

To help you navigate the city, we've chosen the most interesting districts (see the map inside the back cover) and underlined featured venues in colour, according to their location (see below); those venues that are outside these areas are not coloured.

LEBLON

Separated from Ipanema by the Jardim de Ala, Leblon's streets are calm, cool and tree-lined, while Rua Dias Ferreira is about the smartest strip in the city, boasting restaurants such as Zuka (see p052) and Sushi Leblon (see p054) and boutiques like the Isabela Capeto outlet (T 2540 5232).

CENTRO

Rio's downtown and its commercial and financial engine. Architecturally, it's a mix of the ultra-modern, the modernist and the old Colonial, but if Rio has a historic heart, it is Praça XV de Novembro. Most museums and public buildings are here.

LAGOA

The saltwater lagoon that gives Lagoa its name is stunning, with its backdrop of Corcovado, Cristo Redentor (see p013) and mountains. The lagoon is looped by upmarket apartment blocks and a popular cycling/jogging track. At night, crowds are drawn to the food and drink kiosks, as well as the, often open-air, restaurants.

IPANEMA

Copacabana might have the curves, but Ipanema is the beach to be seen at, particularly Posto 9, from mid-afternoon onwards, where the beautiful people watch the sun set. In the 1960s, the area was a bohemian haunt; now, it's home to the swankiest bars, fanciest restaurants and the most expensive real estate.

COPACABANA

The opening of the Copacabana Palace (see p017) in 1923 announced the arrival of this district as an international resort. But by the 1970s, it had started to become a victim of its own success. Now, it is a tourist trap and the beach road, Avenida Atlântica, is lined with restaurants happy to take advantage of visitors straight off the plane. The beach itself is perfect, but Copacabana is due for rehabilitation.

SANTA TERESA

With its rickety trams (bonde) and streets full of fading mansions, tumbling down cobbled streets on a hill, high above the city, Santa Teresa is pretty, verging on cute. But, just like Lapa, it still has some edge. It's more bohemian than Lapa, with a significant artistic community. Now that it's becoming a tourist draw, a number of small hotels are popping up in the area.

LAPA

Just down the hill from Santa Teresa lies Rio's up-and-coming quarter, Lapa. Its fine 19th-century mansions fell into disarray with the exodus of the Carioca elite to the beaches. In the 1920s, it had a reputation as Rio's Montmartre, bohemians and artists mixing with hookers and hard men. Today, it's being revitalised as a nightlife draw. Yet the buildings remain shabby and the clientele a mixed bag: the Leblon cool crowd and middle-aged couples looking to samba the old-fashioned way.

LANDMARKS

THE SHAPE OF THE CITY SKYLINE

In the 1930s, Rio put a three-storey statue of Christ (see p013) on top of a mountain overlooking the city. It quickly became one of the best-known civic symbols in the world. Not that Rio really needed it. The lush mound of Sugar Loaf (see p010) and the gentle curve of Copacabana were already visual cues for this city of supra-natural beauty and high glamour. For Rio has one of the finest physical berths of any city and images of its mountains and beaches are instantly recognisable. The built environment also offers up recognisable clues and markers: the waves of Roberto Burle Marx's mosaic-tiled Copacabana Promenade (see p014), Arcos de Lapa aqueduct (Rua Lélio Gama, T 2242 2354) and Oscar Niemeyer's Museu de Arte Contemporânea de Niterói (see p065).

Much of the city is determinedly modern – a silly confection like Copacabana Palace (see p017) is a rarity here. Rio created an entire waterfront in the 1950s, the Parque do Flamengo, which is home to two startling contemporary landmarks: Museu de Arte Moderna (see p076) and the Second World War Memorial (see p012). Another unmistakable feature of Rio is the *favelas*: shanty townships that tumble down the hills towards the sea. These are monumental, no-go ghettos, which reverse the normal logic that prime real estate gets the best views. One thing's for sure, when you're in Rio, it'll never let you forget it.

For all addresses, see Resources.

Sugar Loaf (Pão de Açúcar)

This distinctive landmark rises 396m above Guanabara Bay in Urca, a lovely area of small, shaded streets and early 20th-century domestic architecture. Sugar Loaf is a popular climb, but you may prefer to take a cable car to Morro da Urca (220m), with its restaurant and open-air theatre, then on to the peak. *Avenida Pasteur 520, T 2461 2700, www.bondinho.com.br*

Second World War Memorial

Parque do Flamengo is 50 acres of landfill, stretching from the airport, right round to Botafogo Bay, and passing through Glória, Catete and Flamengo. Landscaped in the mid-1960s, it was the labour of landscape architect Roberto Burle Marx, and is one of his most ambitious projects in Rio. At the park's northern limits you will find the Museu de Arte Moderna (see p076), and this considerably affecting and dignified monument (above), built to commemorate those young servicemen who died in the Second World War. Designed by Hélio Ribas Marinho and Marcos Konder Neto, the site also includes a museum, mausoleum, the Tomb of the Unknown Soldier and a small lake, as well as sculptures by Alfredo Ceschiatti and Anísio Araújo de Medeiros.
Avenida Infante Dom Henrique 75,
T 2240 1283

Cristo Redentor

The 38m-high, art deco statue of Christ the Redeemer sits 693m above Rio on Corcovado. This massive figure, which is lovely close up, ranks among the top international civic icons and, like New York's Empire State Building and Sydney Opera House, it is instantly identifiable. Designed by artist Carlos Oswald, hands and head sculpted by Paul Landowski, it was installed in 1931 (engineer Heitor da Silva Costa was in charge of the project). It faces towards Sugar Loaf (see p010), with its left arm pointing towards the Maracanã Stadium (see p089) and its right stretching out to Leblon. The statue can be reached with relative ease, and very pleasantly, by road or track, through the Floresta da Tijuca (p093).

Trem do Corcovado, Rua Cosme Velho 513, T 2558 1329, www.corcovado.org.br

Copacabana Promenade

Just about the best-known landscape architect of the 20th century, Roberto Burle Marx worked alongside Brazil's great modernists, Lúcio Costa and Oscar Niemeyer, developing complementary curvilinear abstractions in concrete and plant life. He landscaped Brasília, also worked in Caracas and Miami, and in Rio he landscaped the Parque do Flamengo (Avenida Infante Dom Henrique), as well as the gardens of pretty much every significant modern building in the city, including Palácio Gustavo Capanema (see p072), Museu de Arte Moderna (see p076), Catédral Metropolitana (see p077) and also the Petrobrás building (see p074). But he will be best remembered for the 5km of wavy patterns, created in mosaic tiles, which snake along the promenade beside Copacabana beach (above).

HOTELS

WHERE TO STAY AND WHICH ROOMS TO BOOK

In truth, Rio is not blessed with a tremendous number of fine or interesting hotels. Copacabana Palace (see opposite) remains the preferred accommodation for the visiting great and good, as it has been for more than 80 years. Caesar Park (see po26) and the Sofitel Rio Palace (see po21) offer similar high levels of service, fixtures and fittings. There's nothing here that you'd call a boutique hotel. The Marina All Suites (see po20) is a sophisticated all-suite operation, as the name suggests, with a very fashionable bar and restaurant, and a fantastic situation in Leblon. While, Orla Copacabana Hotel (see po22) and Portinari Design Hotel (see po24) offer more contemporary design at affordable prices.

A scaled-down version of Alan Faena's Faena Hotel + Universe in Buenos Aires (Martha Salotti 445, T 00 54 11 4010 9000) was set to arrive here, but Faena decided against it. Rio's loss. However, it seems that there could be a version of São Paulo's small, but perfectly formed, Fasano (Rua Vittorio Fasana 88, T 00 55 11 3896 4077), by architects Isay Weinfeld and Marcio Kogan.

First-time visitors want to stay in Copacabana, for the elegant curve of the beach and its vivid display of flesh and frolicking. Both are fun to look at. But it is Ipanema and Leblon, with their more sophisticated beach life and easy access to dining, drinking and shopping opportunities, which are our favoured spots.

For all addresses and room rates, see Resources.

Copacabana Palace

Since it opened, just over 80 years ago, this hotel has built up a reputation as being Rio's grandest, although that took a battering during the 1970s and 1980s. It was designed by a French architect, Joseph Gire, to rival Hôtel Negresco (T 00 33 4 9316 6400) and the InterContinental Carlton (T 00 33 4 9306 4006), the twin jewels of the Riviera. When Orient-Express took over, towards the end of the 1980s, it received a much-needed facelift. For a superb view, go for a Penthouse Suite with private veranda. Poolside Suites are also pretty nifty, and the Superior Beach View Rooms (overleaf), on the third and fourth floors, are spacious. Its Cipriani restaurant is one of the best in the city and there's a fantastic rooftop pool and tennis court.
Avenida Atlântica 1702, T 2548 7070, www.copacabanapalace.com.br

Marina All Suites

This hotel is the work of a group of three local architects, who took over an existing hotel building, which had six rooms on each floor, and put in three suites on each floor instead. With Giselle Bündchen and Arnold Schwarzeneggar as guests, this was a smart move. There are 38 suites in total, but the eight design suites are the stars of the show. Check into the Âmbar Suite (above) or treat yourself to a night or two in the Diamante Suite, which might just be the best in the city. There's a lovely rooftop pool and a movie theatre, where you can kick back with your pals and watch a DVD. The Bar d'Hôtel (see p059) is the most glamorous little drinking den in Rio and the fine French restaurant, Café d'Hôtel (see p034), has lovely sea views. *Avenida Delfim Moreira 696, T 2540 4990, www.marinaallsuites.com.br*

Sofitel Rio Palace

Frank Sinatra once stayed and played at this hotel, but if that's not good enough for you, it has also had a $25m renovation since then and now rivals Caesar Park (see p026) and Copacabana Palace (see p017) for luxurious fixtures and fittings. It also boasts a better location than the Palace, at the pleasanter end of Copacabana beach. Smart design means that all 388 rooms get at least a partial beach view and all have balconies and the deluxe rooms guarantee you a full ocean view. But here's the really neat thing, there are two rooftop pools, one to make the most of the morning sun, the other to allow you to appreciate the afternoon sun (above). *Avenida Atlântica 4240, T 2525 1232, www.sofitel.com*

Orla Copacabana Hotel

This mid-budget hotel opened in 2001, and is housed in what resembles a metal-skinned 1980s office block; one that actually delivers a lot of style for the money. There are 'Barcelona' chairs and big art in the narrow lobby and a smart little bar and restaurant. The hotel also has a great location: at the right end of Copacabana beach, in easy walking distance of Ipanema's smartest shopping streets and beach. It's not big on service, or balconies, but it does have a great rooftop pool (right) and bar. The Orla is either full of budget-minded teams of fashion professionals shooting in the city (Rio, after all, is like one huge film set), or the just plain fashionable. All 115 rooms are very well furnished, with large granite bathrooms. Choose a deluxe ocean view room or the Master Suite (above).
Avenida Atlântica 4122, T 2525 2425, www.orlahotel.com.br

Portinari Design Hotel

A block back from Orla Copacabana Hotel (see p022) is the Portinari, another chic but affordable establishment. Each of the 11 floors and 66 rooms were tackled by different local architects and designers before the opening in early 2004, like the third-floor Executive Suite (right) by Cadas Abranches. Inevitably, there's a danger that the Portinari might feel a little over-designed, but even the second-floor suite by Gustavo and Sandra Peña is a gem, despite its lowly position. Indeed, all of the rooms and suites have their own charms. There are no direct beach views, but it's just a short stroll from here into Ipanema. If you decide to eat at the hotel, The Brodowski Restaurant is an excellent rooftop dining area. The tableware depicts paintings by Brazilian artist Cândido Portinari, who the hotel is named after.
Rua Francisco Sá 17, T 3222 8800,
www.portinaridesignhotel.com.br

Caesar Park

Situated in possibly the best location of any Rio hotel, right on the beachfront and in the heart of the Ipanema action, many would consider Caesar Park superior to the more celebrated Copacabana Palace (see p017). The 23-storey hotel underwent a major and well-handled renovation and all rooms are now well-equipped with flat-screen televisions and other technological treats. A Deluxe Room (above) gets an ocean view, while the junior suites offer up Ipanema and Copacabana. Galani, the restaurant on the 23rd floor, offers great views and fine international food, although Saturday lunchtimes are given over to *feijoada* (pork and black bean stew) on the second floor. Caesar Park has a rooftop pool, but also offers beach security, so there's no reason not to head out to the most fashionable beach anywhere.
Avenida Vieira Souto 460, T 2525 2525, www.caesarpark-rio.com

Brava Hotel

About 105 miles and two hours' drive north of Rio is Búzios, 'Brazil's St Tropez', which it's been known as ever since Brigitte Bardot dubbed it that two decades ago, when it was just a small fishing village (an unpleasant brass statue commemorates her influence on the town's development). Most of the accommodation is based in *pousadas*, the Portuguese take on bed and breakfast; the exception is this 30-room boutique hotel. The architecture is a strange, but pleasing, adobe modern, as is revealed in these poolside images (above, right and overleaf). Small and romantic, it has its own helipad, and golf cars take guests to the beach, 150m away. Although stylish, a smidgen of the Sofitel Rio Palace (see p021) or Caesar Park (see p026) sophistication wouldn't go amiss.
Rua 17, Lote 14, Quadra O Praia Brava, Armação dos Búzios, T 22 2623 5943, www.buziosonline.com.br/bravahotel

The Pool, Brava Hotel, Búzios

24 HOURS
SEE THE BEST OF THE CITY IN JUST ONE DAY

No other city can match Rio's place and position, not even Sydney, San Francisco or Cape Town. Long golden beaches, mountains clad in lush greenery, parks and lakes – Rio has them all. However you look at it, Rio is truly blessed, and the best way to look at it is from on high. Sugar Loaf (see p010) and Corcovado, lofty eyrie of the hulking art deco Cristo Redentor (see p013), offer spectacular views over the city – and both peaks are accessible by train or cable car, which makes things easy.

The views are no less spectacular from the most famous beaches in the world, Copacabana and Ipanema (see p038), which also have the most famous beach life and beachwear in the world. Copacabana's gentle arc makes it the more beautiful of the beaches, but it's beset by lazy, predictable establishments, serving lazy, predictable tourists. To avoid this, head for Ipanema and Leblon (see opposite), which is where the smart set, indigenous and in transit, sun themselves – and in very little.

The citizens of Rio are ever in motion, jogging, roller-blading, cycling, kicking or spiking something, from angelic sun-blessed little tikes to chestnut-brown ancients playing beach volleyball in the morning before the crowds and *poseurs* arrive. The urge to join the flow and constant motion is hard to resist. So don't. If you want to see Rio at its best, you need to keep moving. Here's how. *For all addresses, see Resources.*

08.00 Leblon Beach

Most of Rio's best hotels are in Leblon or Ipanema and so, if you're staying here, the perfect start to the day is a brisk jog along Leblon's *calçadão* (a large pavement or promenade) towards Ipanema. As you go, admire the patterns on the pavements, not the work of Roberto Burle Marx (see p014), but still worthy of some attention. Leblon Beach is separated from Ipanema Beach by Jardim de Alah, a canal and gardens, but otherwise the two areas are largely indistinguishable. Watch the beach come to life with early morning games of *voleibol* (volleyball), *frescobal* (beach tennis) and *futebol* (football). After your run, get changed and head for breakfast at the Marina All Suites hotel (see p034), and on your way there, take in the view of Morro Dois Irmãos (above), looming large and lovely in the west.

09.00 Café d'Hôtel

This prime Leblon breakfast spot at the Marina All Suites (see p020) is small but perfectly realised, right down to local designer Lenny Niemeyer's staff uniform of aprons, baggy pants and Converse All Stars. The interior is expertly re-imagined *belle époque* and the tile flooring, which references the patterned pavements outside, is a nice touch. Prepare for the day ahead with granola, yogurt, papaya and pastries on the terrace overlooking the beach. The coffee, selected by barista Isabella Raposeiras, is among the best in the city. If you happen to be staying at the Marina All Suites, or just passing later on, the café's enormous afternoon tea is also a delight. All this, of course, will mean another very long run the next morning. *Avenida Delfim Moreira 696, T 2172 1100, www.marinaallsuites.com.br*

10.00 Lagoa Rodrigo de Freitas

Take a short taxi ride north to this lovely saltwater lagoon, flanked by the swanky apartment blocks of Lagoa and Gávea and beyond those, the mountains of Rio, including Corcovado and Cristo Redentor (see p013). What we're here for is the 8km cycling and walking path around the lake. Pick up a bike (you can rent one for about R$6 an hour) near the Parque Brigadeiro Faria Lima, which is on the west side, and start looping the loop. If you fancy an early lunch, head to the north of Lagoa and try Olympe (T 2539 4542), the recently reopened restaurant belonging to French chef Claude Troisgros.

12.30 Jardim Botânico

Ordered by Emperor Dom João VI two centuries ago, the Jardim Botânico is a little (or, at 1.5 sq km, maybe not so little) slice of Atlantic rainforest bang in the heart of Rio. The gardens contain more than 6,200 tropical species of flora. The garden and its palm-lined avenues seemingly disappear into the Mata Atlântica forest. We suggest you stay firmly within the boundaries of the park and enjoy the lake with its Vitória Régia water lilies, which are over one metre tall. When it comes to eating, there's a good outdoor café here, but we recommend you move on to Guimas (see opposite) instead. *Rua Jardim Bontânico 1008, T 3874 1808, www.jbrj.gov.br*

13.30 Guimas

A very superior sort of *boteco* (open-air restaurant), Guimas (above) has been serving Rio's foodies with top-notch cuisine for more than 20 years. Located south-west of Jardim Botânico, it's the perfect spot for lunch – try the delicious codfish lasagne. If you decide to stretch lunch out until well into the afternoon before heading over to Ipanema, who are we to argue? After all, Guimas has a fine selection of wine and spirits and knows how to use it. It's also known as a spot where the diners get more interesting as the day draws on.
Rua José Roberto Macedo Soares 5,
T 2259 7996

15.00 Ipanema Beach

If you didn't spend too long over lunch, you might just about find time to squeeze in watching the sun set on Ipanema Beach. First developed in 1894, but really hitting its swing in the 1960s, this beach is where the city's beautiful people come to top up their tans. The section you want to head for is Posto 9, off Rua Vinícius de Moraes. Once the meeting place of Rio's bohemian left, it's now the most desirable pitch for the golden sunset hour (or any other hour, for that matter). The beautiful people are plentiful here and plenty beautiful too, although there are still a few old hippies to contend with. Once you've had your fill of the dying light, it's time to head for a bar. A few of your beach mates may join you – especially if you ask nicely.

20.00 Garota de Ipanema

This bar is on the site of Bar Velso, where composer Tom Jobim and Brazilian poet and songwriter Vinícius de Moraes wrote bossa nova lite standard 'The Girl from Ipanema' (for their efforts Jobim got an airport named after him and de Moraes just this street). The first few lines are written on the wall here – in case you've somehow managed to forget them. Inevitably, given its location and the link, the bar is a bit of a tourist draw, but it's a friendly and very pleasant post-sunset spot for *kibes* (bulgar wheat and minced beef) and *chopps* (weak, ice-cold Brazilian beer). You simply can't go to Ipanema and not come here – it wouldn't be right.
Rua Vinícius de Moraes 134, T 2522 0340

URBAN LIFE

CAFÉS, RESTAURANTS, BARS AND NIGHTCLUBS

Cariocas are dedicated to living city life as if they were nowhere near a city. By day, the beaches of Ipanema, Leblon and Copacabana are crammed with the young and lithe showing off their *bundas* (butts) in *fio dentals* (string bikinis; literally, 'dental floss'). By night, the bars and restaurants are packed out until the early hours, with no sense that the working day is just a few hours away. And, come the weekend, the Cariocas really go to town. The traditional focus of Rio nightlife has been laidback and leafily lovely Leblon and neighbouring, if slightly more frantic, Ipanema. They still haven't shaken off their history as sixties boho hangouts and even the smartest venues keep things low key.

The hot dining zone of the moment is Leblon's Rua Dias Ferreira, a strip of stark, modern boxes dedicated to international cuisine. The best drinking and dancing is way across town in Lapa, where 19th-century mansions, long abandoned by the Carioca elite (lured away by the developing beach communities), are being converted into raucous samba zones, dance halls and drinking dens. For now, everywhere is elegant decay, but there are the first signs of a corporate clean-up and bland-out, so get there soon. Avenida Mem de Sá is the swaying, shambolic heart of Lapa's scene, but make Rio Scenarium (see p044) on Rua do Lavradio (now emerging as the place to pick up mid-century design) your first port of call. *For all addresses, see Resources.*

Espaço Cultural Maurice Valansi
This quirky combination of bar and café in Botafogo, is also part bookshop and photography gallery, as well as playing host to the Musea de Cadeira, an amazing collection of chairs. It's this that makes it just about the oddest nightspot in the city (and Rio has some very, very peculiar hangouts), but we love it. Where else can you go to sup cocktails and tuck into tasty crêpes or sushi, read books and admire classics by Charles and Ray Eames, Hans J Wegner, Harry Bertoia or Frank Gehry, which are just dangling from the ceiling? Inevitably, the gallery space also runs an annual competition for chair design.
Rua Martins Ferreira 48, T 2527 4044

Forneria Rio
Rogério Fasano and chief architectural
accomplice Isay Weinfeld bring their
warm South American modernism to
Rio with this Ipanema version of their
São Paulo *sanduicheria*. Fine paninis,
vintage Italian movie posters and the
open airy space, make it perfect for
both dinner and street-side cocktails.
Rua Aníbal de Mendonça 112,
T 2540 8045

Rio Scenarium

If you do anything while you're in Rio, you have to pay a visit to this comely, if rather crumbling, 19th-century, three-storey warehouse. With around 2,000 antiques and oddities, display cabinets and old chandeliers scattered casually about, it's easy to imagine that Rio Scenarium began life as an antiques store — yet it now plays host to bands playing samba, *chorino* (a vocally led style of 19th-century Brazilian music) and more. It's the eccentric anchor tenant of Centro's very lively night scene, and the upper-floor balconies are the ideal vantage point from which to watch the wayward street life passing by below. *Rua do Lavradio 20, T 3147 9005, www.rioscenarium.com.br*

Juice Co

Cariocas are notoriously health-conscious, after all, maintaining those beautiful beach bods takes time and effort. This sharp-looking Leblon restaurant and bar is a startling modern box, on a tree-lined street of 19th-century townhouses. It serves up all manner of healthy organic fare, devised by Dutch chef Jeroen van den Bos – try the yogurt-honey-orange-banana 'energy cocktail'. Thankfully, van den Bos is just as serious about his meats and carbohydrates, so you can refuel properly and in style here.
Avenida General San Martin 889,
T 2294 0048

Academia da Cachaça

Many Cariocas have developed a taste for *caipiroskas* (a vodka-based bastardisation of the Brazilian favourite), but traditional caipirinhas (made with lime, sugar, ice and a potent cane liquor cachaça) are still regarded as the Brazilian national drink. Academia da Cachaça, only 11 years old but now a Rio institution (despite being slightly short on atmosphere), celebrates the local hooch, holding and serving 500 different varieties. It also mixes, almost indisputably, the best caipirinha in town and the restaurant, which specialises in North East Brazilian cuisine, is very sound (try the fillet steak cooked in ginger). *Rua Conde Bernadotte 26, T 2239 1542*

Estrela da Lapa

The Lapa nightlife, the most vibrant in Rio, has taken root in what was formerly a sketchy network of shady side streets, lined with faded mansion houses. While Rio Scenarium (see p044) and Carioca da Gema (see p058) are still unsettled and shambolic spaces, Estrela da Lapa has been given a thorough refurbishment. It is now grand, lovely and very clean with an upstairs terrace (above) overlooking a dance floor and stage. Yet it can seem to be just a little corporate and anodyne, with none of the sweat and tight spaces that distinguish the best of the Lapa scene.
Avenida Mem de Sá 69, T 2507 6686

Bar Luiz Beach Kiosk
Bar Luiz (T 2262 6900) first opened in
1887 and has been in Rua da Carioca
since it moved there in 1927. Little has
changed, from the original 1920s tiled
floor and wooden tables, to the Austro-
German food and cold beers it serves.
But it's now branched out, opening this
kiosk (below), a little slice of updated
Americana on Copacabana beach.
www.barluiz.com.br

Mil Frutas

Next door to the Louis Vuitton store on Rio's choicest little shopping street, Mil Frutas peddles deliciously fruity ice cream to the Ipanema locals. The recipes, which originated in Renata Saboya's kitchen in 1998, include exotic Brazilian fruits and potent scoops such as absinthe and sake with mombin (a yellow plum-like fruit); there are 160 flavours in all. Great salads, sandwiches and wraps are also on offer and you can take a seat on the store-front patio to watch the girls from Ipanema pass by en route to the neighbouring boutiques. *Rua Garcia d'Avila 134A, T 2521 1384, www.milfrutas.com.br*

Devassa

Owned by the king of the Rio night scene, Marcelo do Rio, Devassa, which is a micro-brewery, serves up locally produced beers that are the best in the city. The bar is in Leblon and is, essentially, a re-imagined boho bistro, or a Brazilian *boteco* anyway, with wooden tables, mosaic-tiled floors (more Burle Marx references, see p014) and big open windows to let in the night air. It might be a confection, but it is a very successful one and it draws a crowd that cares more about the fine cold beer and fine hot food than it does about the absolute authenticity of the surroundings.
Avenida General San Martin 1241,
T 2540 6087, www.devassa.com.br

Zuka

Rua Dias Ferreira is fast emerging as Rio's choicest restaurant strip, chock full of fashionable restaurants, and Zuka is probably one of the best. It's housed in a modernist cube, with marbled walls and a sunken kitchen area, where 27-year-old chef, Ludmila Soeiro, cooks up Italian food with Asian touches on the charcoal grill. You'll get the best tortellini in Brazil here, so they say, and the roasted bananas, served in blackened skins, with vanilla ice cream and hot sugar-cane molasses, is a dessert par excellence. But, as well as the fine food, Zuka is all about eating among the city's young and fabulous, on Rio's most quietly fabulous little strip. *Rua Dias Ferreira 233, T 3205 7154*

Confeitaria Colombo

This fantastic *fin-de-siècle* tearoom makes for a strange and incongruous sight on an undistinguished side street in Centro. Go just to check out the huge jacaranda-framed mirrors, marble-top counters and beautiful French stained-glass in the ceiling above the three-storey, atriumed interior. In its heyday, Colombo was the spot for top Cariocas and they are now returning in droves for afternoon coffee and intrigue. The first-floor dining room is a popular spot for the traditional Saturday *feijoada* (pork and black bean stew), but you could make afternoon ice cream a more regular treat.
*Rua Gonçalves Dias 32, T 2232 2300,
www.confeitariacolombo.com.br*

Sushi Leblon

This has to be the best sushi place in town, although Manekineko (T 2540 7424), which is owned by the Zuka crew (see p052), and on the same stretch of Rua Dias Ferreira, is also a top draw for lovers of Japanese cuisine with a Euro twist. And, while Sushi Leblon's shrimp with foie gras gets all the attention, all your raw-fish favourites are handled expertly here. The interior's clean, light-on-the-lacquer look is as smart a take on modern Japanese as the food, all of which makes this place a fearsomely fashionable fixture for the Leblon luvvies.
Rua Dias Ferreira 256, T 2512 7830

Caroline Café

This café is similar to Devassa (see p051), being a two-storey house, which is close to the botanical gardens. It's also another Marcelo do Rio number (Melt, his low-key but ultra-fashionable place in Leblon, was undergoing a much-needed refit as we went to press). As with Devassa, Caroline reworks the traditional *boteco* to great effect. It succeeds in pulling in those who would normally never leave the environs of Leblon and Ipanema. They make the journey here specially, because they love the ambience of its pavement patio.
Rua JJ Seabra 10, T 2540 0705

Garcia e Rodrigues

A two-storey Parisian gastro-complex, comprising deli, patisserie, restaurant, café, cookbook shop, kitchenwares stockist and restaurant, this eaterie is situated in the heart of Leblon. The chefs have domesticated the French cooking somewhat, but it remains a popular spot with French locals and visitors. It's also the place to go if you're hankering after something very special in the way of breads, as there are 30 types of baguettes and rolls on offer, along with wines and cheeses. Everything you need to set you up for a delicious picnic.
Avenida Ataúlfo de Paiva 1251, T 3206 4120, www.garciaerodrigues.com.br

Carioca da Gema

The bar/restaurant that first fired up the high-octane Lapa nightlife scene, Carioca da Gema is an old colonial pile on Lapa's main drag. Friday and Saturday nights are samba nights and definitely the time to go. It has a reputation for presenting the best samba and *chorinho* acts around, so be prepared for plenty of sweaty motion and, as the bar is not large, much intimacy with strangers. It's possibly just as well that there's always a taxi-cab waiting, and also that under-18s are barred entry.
Avenida Mem de Sá 79, T 2221 0043, www.barcariocadagema.com.br

Bar d'Hotel

This second-floor bar and restaurant at the Marina All Suites hotel (see p020) is Rio's most fashionable bar, where the beautiful people park their *bundas* (butts) for flirtation and frolics with a beach view, the coolest people arriving after 10pm. The food is Italian and fine, with the waiter bringing the menu over on a chalk blackboard, but it's the cocktails that have really built the bar's reputation. Try the sake caipirinha or one of the lumpily satisfying passion-fruit versions. But for goodness' sake, get a tan before you go, as pale and interesting isn't going to cut it. *Avenida Delfim Moreira 696, T 2540 4990*

00

This restaurant and nightclub is attached to the Gávea planetarium. The food served up is eclectic and superb, and the music, should you tire of samba and bossa nova, is heavy on the house and R&B. Indeed, with its chic international decor, this is one of the few Rio nightspots that doesn't do the vernacular thing and, frankly, could be anywhere in the world (weather permitting – 00's prize asset is its terrace).

Sunday is a very big night here, pulling in many of Rio's most dedicated partygoers.
Planetário de Gávea, Avenida Padre Leonel França 240, T 2540 8041
www.00site.com.br

INSIDER'S GUIDE

DOROTHEÉ POTOCKI, JEWELLERY DESIGNER

With a Polish father and Swedish mother and peripatetic from birth, jewellery designer Dorotheé Potocki had lived in Rome, Athens, Geneva, Moscow, Warsaw and New York before studying design in Geneva and then moving to Buenos Aires. She moved on to Rio in 2002 and established her own jewellery line, using only local craftsmen and Brazilian stones. Now living in Ipanema, Potocki recommends Posto 9 as the loveliest slice of Rio beach life, and the best place to be in the afternoon 'to play cards, swim and play racquets when the sun sets.' She likes concept store and café Clube Chocolate in São Conrado (Estrada da Gávea 899, T 3322 3733): 'plenty of good Brazilian designers and it's nice for lunch.' Lulu (Rua Visconde de Carandaí 2, T 2294 7830), an Italian restaurant in Jardim Botânico, is 'a little three-storey house on a quiet street, but the top-floor terrace has amazing views of Cristo Redentor (see p013). And the food is delicious.'

For the definitive Carioca good night out, Potocki is a big fan of Carioca da Gema (see p058), the bar that kick-started Lapa's regeneration. 'A great, traditional place to eat and dance forró, chorinho, samba, with people of all social backgrounds and ages.' For a more sophisticated evening out, try Bar d'Hotel (see p059) on the second floor of the Marina All Suites hotel (see p020). 'You can have a lovely dinner watching the ocean. They do the best caipirinhas, the decor is lovely and the people are pretty.'

ARCHITOUR

A GUIDE TO RIO'S ICONIC BUILDINGS

If Brasília (see p100) is the emphatic concrete evidence of the Brazilian embrace of modernism, then it's in Rio that you see how and why the style developed. The work of Oscar Niemeyer, in particular, shows how much the Brazilian style is a Carioca construct, born of sun, mountains and beaches, and the sensuality of a life lived half-naked and close to the sea. Born in 1907, Niemeyer is the last surviving modernist, and is only now getting recognition for nearly 80 years of work. In Rio, his ambitious and optimistic architecture uses arches, curves and cantilevers to make concrete appear light and fluid, in a natural response to the landcape.

From the 1930s through to the military coup of the mid-1960s, Niemeyer, Lúcio Costa and a whole wave of Brazilian architects were enlisted into grand civic and national modernisation programmes. In Rio, whole areas of the city were knocked down and new areas of land created, where once there had been only water. Niemeyer exiled himself to Europe after the coup, but he returned to Rio in the late 1970s and his most famous work was finished here in 1996, when he was almost 90: the Museu de Arte Contemporânea (opposite) in Niterói, across the Guanabara Bay, which is as whimsical, fantastic and beguiling as anything he had produced previously. As we write, Niemeyer is still active, working on two churches and a ferry station, also in Niterói.
For all addresses, see Resources.

Museu de Arte Contemporânea

In a documentary on Oscar Niemeyer, Belgian film-maker Marc-Henri Wajnberg imagined the fantastical contemporary art museum swooping over Rio, almost dislodging Cristo Redentor (see p013), before settling on a narrow peninsula in Niterôi, 15km from the city. It's the obvious metaphor for Niemeyer's design, which resembles a flying-saucer and does seem to hover above the ground. Although it's tempting to write off the 1996 building as camp retro-futurism, to see it shining bright, light and white in the sun, looking otherworldly but also right at home, is to understand Niemeyer's intentions. (The real shame of it is that the budget for the project was little more than R$5m. And it shows in some of the finishing.)
Mirante da Boa Viagem, Niterói,
T 2620 2400

Sambódromo

In 1940, President Getulio Vargas, the revolutionary-turned-dictator, was keen on massive modernisation programmes. He ordered a 4km, 12-lane highway to be cut through Rio, which was to be lined with identical 22-storey office blocks. Few were actually built, but it left plenty of space for Niemeyer's massive samba stadium, the Sambódromo, designed and built in only 110 days in time for the 1984

Carnaval. More a series of different stadia and spaces strung out across half a mile, it is the venue for the main Carnaval parade, when 14 samba schools wiggle and stomp around to the beat of 200-400 drummers, in front of a crowd of 30,000 people.
Rua Marquês de Sapucaí

Palácio Gustavo Capanema

In 1936, Brazil's Minister for Education and Health, Gustavo Capanema, decided he wanted a ministry building. He went to Lúcio Costa, who began the work but, dissatisfied with his design, invited Le Corbusier, who had yet to build anything substantial in Europe, to come to Rio and act as consultant on the project. It was Le Corbusier who suggested a strict modernist block. Oscar Niemeyer, who had just joined Costa's practice, came up with his own adaptations, shifting the orientation of the building, lifting it 40 feet off the ground on marble-covered pillars, and adding moveable sunshades. The Brazilian painter, Candido Portinari, designed the extravagant tile work, while Roberto Burle Marx added a roof garden. Palácio Gustavo Capanema is one of the most important, influential and successful modernist buildings anywhere.
Rua da Imprensa 16

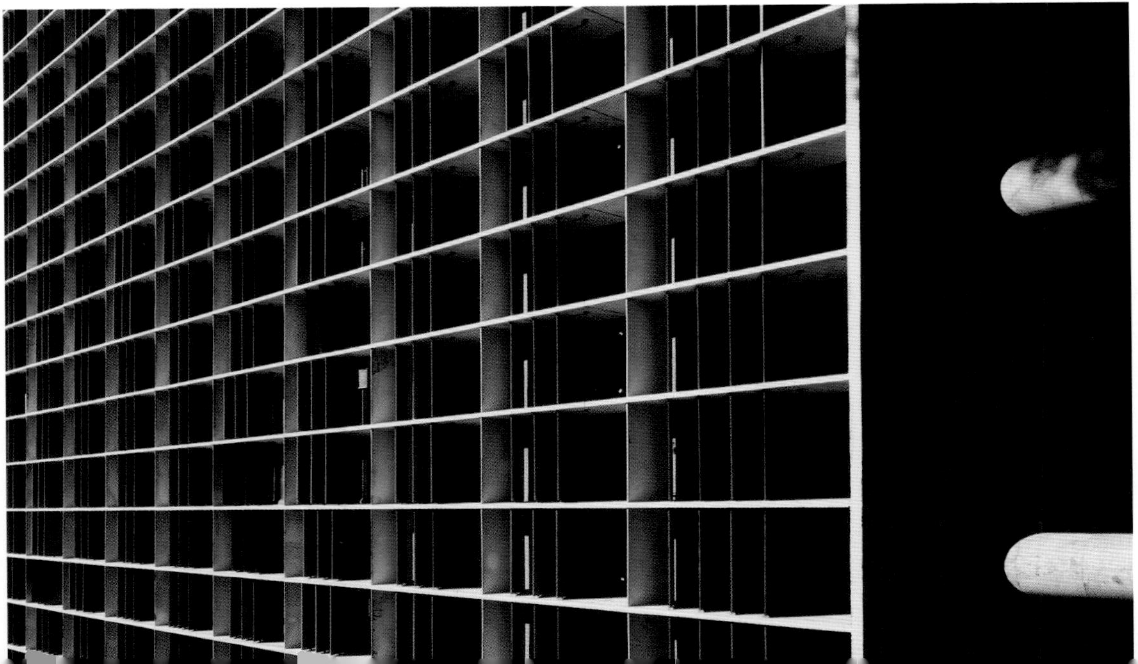

The Petrobrás Building
Built in 1969, the headquarters for the state-owned oil company, is 27 storeys of corporate muscle in concrete and steel. The design, by Roberto Gandolfi, with its metal skin and pillared recesses (allowing for Roberto Burle Marx's 'hanging gardens'), makes this one of the most interesting, beguiling, if not to say confounding, corporate slabs.
Rua Lélio Gama 65

Museu de Arte Moderna (MAM)

A building that truly struts its stuff, MAM sits high and proud at the northern end of the Parque do Flamengo. It was designed in 1953 by another Lúcio Costa acolyte, Affonso Eduardo Reidy, who also worked on Palácio Gustavo Capanema (see p072), but it wasn't completed till 1958. The giant pillars and trusses that support the main building allow for huge expanses of glass and a vast interior space free of structural obstructions and interferences. This makes for great views of the surrounding sea and mountains and Roberto Burle Marx's landscaped gardens. Some complain that it's not a great space to look at art, but it remains a fresh and powerful design.
Avenida Infante Dom Henrique 85, T 2240 4944, www.mamrio.com.br

Catédral Metropolitana

Opened in 1976 and 12 years in the making, its real name is Catédral de São Sebastiao, but it's known as Catédral Metropolitana. The building's design is everything that Oscar Niemeyer's uplifting cathedral in Brasília (see p100) is not. Cariocas have little affection for this dark, brooding and, frankly, brutal concrete cone, which is associated with the era of the dictators. Visitors, free of such associations, see a great modern cathedral: four enormous latticed sides, 'falling in' on each other and four stunning 60m-high stained-glass windows, topped by a translucent cross in the centre of a circle that measures an impressive 30m in diameter. That it can hold a congregation of 20,000 gives you some sense of the building's scale.
Avenida República do Chile 245,
T 2240 2669, www.catedral.com.br

Parque Guinle

Lúcio Costa, a founding father of Brazilian modernism, wanted this development to root and connect European rationalist architecture to Brazilian vernacular style, while also adapting international style to the Brazilian climate. Built between 1948 and 1954, the three residential towers, Nova Cintra, Bristol and Caledônia (six were originally planned), were part of Rio's first modernist mass housing project. The influence of Le Corbusier is obvious in the *pilotis* (pillars) and the sunscreens. There was, of course, an irony in glazing large buildings and then covering them in sunscreens. However, aesthetically, it looked very sharp indeed, and by adding these sunscreens Costa also built in a little bit of Brazil.
Rua Gago Coutinho 66-68 and Rua Paulo César de Andrade 70 and 106

SHOPPING

THE CITY'S BEST SHOPS AND WHAT TO BUY

The Rio retail scene will never match the sprawling spread of São Paolo, but the super-chic Avenida Ataúlfo de Paiva and Rua Visconde de Pirajá, in Leblon and Ipanema respectively, offer boutiques and mini-malls to a famously glamorous population. Despite popular myth, Cariocas don't spend most of their time in thongs on the beach, and are dedicated shoppers. Perhaps more than in São Paolo, Rio is the place where Brazilian style has been defined. Osklen (see p083), is a Rio-based chain of sporty fashion stores that's become the darling of fashionistas. Of the other local labels, Maria Bonita (see p086) and Isabela Capeto (Rua Dias Ferreira 45, T 2540 5232) best represent the national spirit.

But, before you write off Cariocas as shallow beach bunnies and clothes-horses, know that they're also keen readers, and Rio is littered with fine bookstores. Two of the best are Letras & Expressões (Avenida Ataúlfo de Paiva 1292, T 2511 5085) and Livraria da Travessa (Rua Visconde de Pirajá 572, T 3205 9002), serving up books, mags, CDs and coffee. For contemporary Brazilian music, Copacabana's Modern Sound (Rua Barata Ribeiro 502, T 2548 5005) is a good place to start. By night Lapa may be the centre of the samba scene, but by day, the crumbling 19th-century mansion houses of Rua do Lavradio are home to vintage furniture stores, such as Mercado Moderno (see p081). *For all addresses, see Resources.*

Mercado Moderno

Lapa is still only in the first stages of gentrification and most of its fantastic 19th-century townhouses remain close to rack and ruin. A few have been turned into steamy samba halls, most famously Rio Scenarium (see p044), which began life as an antique store. This place, just a few doors down, headed in the opposite direction. Originally a hip night spot, after an extensive refit in 2005 it reopened as Rio's best 20th-century furniture store. The stock is determinedly mid-century, with a heavy accent on excellent local designers such as Ricardo Fasanello and Sergio Rodrigues. But all the pieces are restored and returned to their original glory by local craftsmen – the patina of age does not wear very well in this city. *Rua do Lavradio 130, T 2508 6083, www.mercadomodernobrasil.com.br*

Antonio Bernardo

Leblon-born Bernardo is Brazil's most respected contemporary jeweller and designer. A second-generation goldsmith and watchmaker, for the past 30 years he has defined and refined his unique way with gold (almost always gold, and unornamented). But Bernardo's quiet, sophisticated and organic designs are as far from blinging baubles as you can imagine. His collection, along with more experimental one-off pieces, produced at his Jardim Botânico atelier, can be seen in a chic in-store shed within his appropriately stark Ipanema store.
Rua Garcia d'Ávila 121, T 2512 7204

Osklen

This is a kind of sportier, Brazilian version of Gap, but much more desirable than that makes it sound. It was set up in 1988 as a snow/surf label by Oskar Metsavaht, the first Brazilian mountaineer to climb Mont Blanc. Osklen now has stores throughout the country, including ten in Rio. It has a playful take on all-year-round sports and casual wear, such as these boots (above), R$449. This has made it a favourite with fashion-minded Cariocas headed for the hills or the beach. It is also an essential stop-off for visiting fashionistas, for an accessible slice of Brazilian chic.
Rua Maria Quitéria 85, T 2227 2911

Atelier Ricardo Fasanello

An iconic piece of Brazilian design, the late Ricardo Fasanello's 'Anel' chair (above), R$4,470, is elegant, simple and functional. It looks great and is also damned comfy. It's not surprising that, with a design CV that includes such iconic pieces as this and the 'Arcos' coffee table, Fasanello's schtick is on the rise. The Espasso store in New York (T 00 1 718 472 0022), which opened in 2002, is dedicated to Brazilian design, and has done much to introduce Fasanello to a wider audience. He died in 1993, but 16 craftsmen are still producing furniture in his Santa Teresa workshop in Rio, overseen by Fasanello's wife, Olivia, and their four children.

Rua do Paraizo 42, T 2232 3164

Loja Novo Desenho

This store occupies a fine little space, designed by Leblon architect Mauricio Nóbrega, within Affonso Eduardo Reidy's fantastic Museu de Arte Moderna (see p076). Designer and design writer Tulio Mariante and his partner Olga Bronstein set up the store at the tail end of 2004. They collected together the best of early 20th-century and contemporary Brazilian design, from furniture to jewellery. It's a small space, but Nóbrega's design makes the most of it and Mariante's revolving edit is joyful, accenting the colour and play in Brazilian design, as seen in these 'Vasos Cenários' (above), R$197 each, designed by Ligia de Medeiros.
Museu de Arte Moderna, Avenida Infante Dom Henrique 85, T 2524 2290

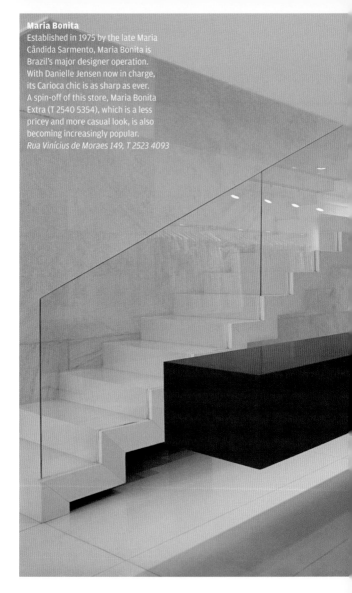

Maria Bonita
Established in 1975 by the late Maria
Cândida Sarmento, Maria Bonita is
Brazil's major designer operation.
With Danielle Jensen now in charge,
its Carioca chic is as sharp as ever.
A spin-off of this store, Maria Bonita
Extra (T 2540 5354), which is a less
pricey and more casual look, is also
becoming increasingly popular.
Rua Vinícius de Moraes 149, T 2523 4093

SPORTS AND SPAS
WORK OUT, CHILL OUT OR JUST WATCH

Brazil has produced more Formula One champions than any other country, bar the United Kingdom, and the late Ayrton Senna is considered one of the greatest in the sport's history. It also has a fair clutch of top tennis players, but the country has become synonymous with one sport. Brazil owns soccer. Outright. The country has won more soccer World Cups than any other nation and has certainly done it with more style. It has produced a string of players known and idolised around the world, from Garrincha, Pele, Zico, through Romario, to Ronaldo and Ronaldinho. And the game played in the famous yellow jerseys has mostly been a mix of grace, intelligence, daring and a fair amount of showboating.

The myth of Brazilian football is that many of its top players pick up their skills playing barefoot footie on the beaches of Rio. And the thing is, it's true. Any stroll along Ipanema or Copacabana beaches will soon leave you slack jawed, watching the city's young girls and boys playing like angels.

And the superannuated beach-volleyball players further illustrate how much physical activity is part of the Carioca lifestyle. Cyclists and joggers flow along Ipanema and Leblon's beachfronts and the newly refurbished cycle track around Lagoa is ringed by good-looking flesh in motion. This seems the very definition of the Carioca spirit: good-looking flesh in motion is what they do best. *For all addresses, see Resources.*

Maracanã Football Stadium

For soccer fans all around the world, this stadium is a Mecca, an enormous shrine, in a city where the game of football really is much more important than religion. It was built to host the 1950 World Cup finals and still holds the record for the greatest recorded crowd attendance at a football match: 199,854. Since then, the capacity has been reduced to 100,000. These days, the game you should be there for is the

Fla-Flu: the local derby that takes place between Flamengo and Fluminese. This is your chance to experience the Maracaña as it's meant to be, with the banging of massed samba drums, incredible noise smoke bombs and flying cups of pee. Of course, any game offers a more restrained version of Maracaña mayhem. And, given the flying pee, this might be a good idea.
Rua Professor Eurico Rabela, T 2568 9962

Maracanã Football Stadium

Jóquei Clube Brasileiro

One of the most beautiful race courses in Brazil, if not the world, the Jóquei Clube is in a spectacular setting on the western side of Lagoa (see p035), surrounded by mountains and overlooked by the Cristo Redentor (see p013). You can't help but wonder how many of the Carioca punters there have prayed for divine intervention as their nags limped home? Built in 1926, the stands hold more than 50,000. They are marvellous structures, if now a little shabby round the edges, while the betting counters in the interior have been lovingly preserved and the introduction of monitors handled with care. Races are four times a week and, for a fee, you can get into the member's area, with bar and table service.
Rua Jardim Botânico 1003, T 2512 9988

Floresta da Tijuca

Rio feels like the most fecund of cities, as if it's struggling to hold back the rainforest into which it was inserted. Indeed, a mere 15 minutes from Copacabana, you find yourself entering the Parque Nacional de Tijuca, a slice of genuine rainforest, which covers 120 sq km. In the mid-19th century, native fauna was reintroduced to the area, in a reforestation programme that was a pioneering act of environmental fixing.

The most domesticated section of the park is Floresta da Tijuca (above), which is noted for its idyllic waterfall, Cascatinha de Taunay. The forest also boasts caves, picnic spots and, thankfully, a number of restaurants. The forest has a well-marked system of trails running through it, to assist the dedicated hiker. If you're really committed, you can always try climbing to the top of Pico de Tijuca (1,022m high).

Ilha Grande

Just a two-and-a-half-hour drive south of
Rio lies this lush, 40km-long, tropical
island, which is just as every kid imagines
a tropical island: rainforests, beaches, big
wooden boats with huge sails, monkeys,
a veritable Neverland. This is born out by
its history involving pirates, smuggling
and the natives, who are said to have even
hunted under water. There are no roads
on the island and, with it being a National
Park, there never will be. The only way to
reach the most popular of its hundred or
so beaches is by schooner, picked up in
the small town of Vila do Abraão, with its
cobbled streets and *pousadas* (bed and
breakfast places). Snorkelling or diving
are the island's most pleasing diversions,
and you can trek, sail or kayak. Our
favourite spot in which to play Peter Pan
and Wendy is Sítio do Lobo (T 2227 4138),
which is a nine-bedroom retreat built on
rocks and buried deep in the forest.

ESCAPES

WHERE TO GO IF YOU WANT TO LEAVE TOWN

Rio is not short of nearby attractions: beaches, islands, mountains, rainforests. Costa Verde, to the west of Rio, is a mess of beautiful highs and lows, which makes for a thrilling drive. A couple of hours west of Rio is Ilha Grande (see p094), one of the country's most beautiful islands, a lush mountain range falling into the sea, fringed with fantastic beaches. There are no roads on the islands and the only way to get to the beaches is by schooner, which is no bad thing. Then there's Paraty, four hours west of Rio, which is something of a colonial theme park, but is impossibly pretty.

Petrópolis is a grand European mountain resort and imperial hideaway, a long way from Europe, but only 70km north of Rio. Once an intellectual hotbed, it's now gaining a reputation as the place where ambitious Brazilian chefs open up small restaurants.

Forever associated with Brigitte Bardot, who decided it was the Brazilian St Tropez in 1964, Búzios (see p028) is the resort that chic Cariocas escape to when Ipanema becomes just too much. The village is now full of boutiques and restaurants, but the real appeal of Búzios is its 25 beaches.

Of course, there's more to Brazil than tropical scenery, golden sands and azure waters. There's also concrete, a lot of concrete. Curitiba, south of São Paulo, and something of a hike, has a reputation as a marvel of modern city planning, while Brasília (see p100) is an essential trip for any committed modernist.

Ilhabela

Around 350km south of Rio, the island of Ilhabela has a long history as a smugglers' hideout and general centre for piratical bad behaviour. Later, it was adopted by the slightly more decorous (but only slightly) São Paulo yachting crew. Since then, the island has established itself as an eco-tourist draw. More than 85 per cent is National Park, with 35km of beaches, a coastal Atlantic rainforest, a UNESCO Biosphere Reserve, mountain peaks and more than 400 waterfalls. The place to stay is DPNY Beach (T 12 3894 2121), a top boutique hotel on the south of the island.

Ilhabela

Brasília

For years, the Brazilian capital was held up as proof of the failures of modernist architecture and also of social planning. Meanwhile, Brasília got on with the job of being a proper city and expanding rapidly, and people are now starting to see the thrill and daring of the city's vision and its architecture. It was Lúcio Costa who came up with the famous aeroplane shape for the city, but the buildings were by Oscar Niemeyer. In Brasília, he mobilised a simple, powerful monumentalism, that had not been seen before in his work and was not to everyone's taste. Now the twin towers and giant domes of the Congress building (left), the elegant arches of the foreign ministry, the stark colonnades of the palaces and the dramatic crowned cone of the cathedral (above) look like a beautiful, brave new world that never was.

Dear Reader, Books by Phaidon are recognised world-wide for their beauty, scholarship and elegance. We invite you to return this card with your name and e-mail address so that we can keep you informed of our new publications, special offers and events. Alternatively, visit us at **www.phaidon.com** to see our entire list of books, videos and stationery. Register on-line to be included on our regular e-newsletters.

Subjects in which I have a special interest

☐ General Non-Fiction   ☐ Art   ☐ Photography   ☐ Architecture   ☐ Design

☐ Fashion   ☐ Music   ☐ Children's   ☐ Food   ☐ Travel

	Mr/Miss/Ms	Initial	Surname
Name			
No./Street			
City			
Post code/Zip code		Country	
E-mail			

This is not an order form. To order please contact Customer Services at the appropriate address overleaf.

Please delete address *not* required before mailing

PHAIDON PRESS INC.

180 Varick Street

New York

NY 10014

PHAIDON PRESS LIMITED

Regent's Wharf

All Saints Street

London N1 9PA

Return address for USA and Canada only

Return address for UK and countries
outside the USA and Canada only

Affix
stamp
here

NOTES

SKETCHES AND MEMOS

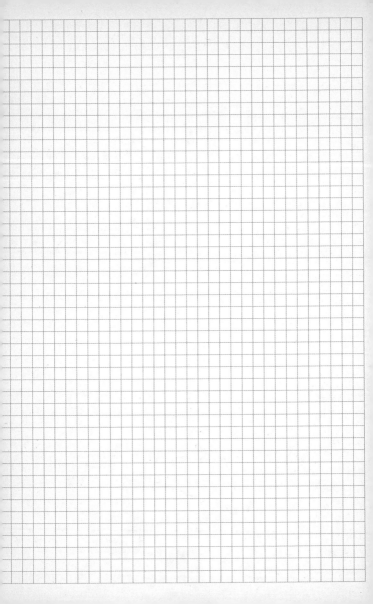

RESOURCES
ADDRESSES AND ROOM RATES

LANDMARKS

009 Arcos de Lapa
Rua Lélio Gama
T 2242 2354

010 Sugar Loaf
(Pão de Açúcar)
Avenida Pasteur 520
T 2461 2700
www.bondinho.com.br

012 Second World
War Memorial
Avenida Infante Dom
Henrique 75,
Parque do Flamengo
T 2240 1283

013 Cristo Redentor
Trem do Corcovado,
Rua Cosme Velho 513
T 2558 1329
www.corcovado.org.br

HOTELS

016 Faena Hotel
+ Universe
Room rates:
double, US$350–US$475
Martha Salotti 445,
Buenos Aires, Argentina
T 00 54 11 4010 9000
www.faenahoteland
universe.com

016 Fasano
Room rates:
double R$1,008
Rua Vittorio Fasana 88,
São Paulo
T 00 55 11 3896 4077
www.fasano.com.br

017 Copacabana Palace
Room rates:
double, R$950;
Superior Beach View,
R$1,302;
Penthouse Suite,
R$4,408–R$5,206
Avenida Atlântica 1702
T 2548 7070
www.copacabanapalace.
com.br

017 Hôtel Negresco
37, Promenade des Anglais,
Nice, France
T 00 33 4 9316 6400
www.hotel-negresco-nice.
com

017 InterContinental
Carlton Hotel
58 Boulevard la Croisette,
Cannes, France
T 00 33 4 9306 4006
www.ichotelsgroup.com

020 Marina All Suites
Room rates:
double, R$720;
Diamante Suite, R$2,000;
Âmbar Suite, R$1,230
Avenida Delfim
Moreira 696
T 2540 4990
www.marinaallsuites.
com.br

021 Sofitel Rio Palace
Room rates:
double, R$470;
Deluxe Room, R$575
Avenida Atlântica 4240
T 2525 1232
www.sofitel.com

022 Orla Copacabana
Room rates:
double, R$260–R$330;
Superior Ocean View,
R$280;
Master Suite, R$560
Avenida Atlântica 4122
T 2525 2425
www.orlahotel.com.br

024 Portinari
Design Hotel
Room rates:
double, R$288;
Executive Suite, R$315;
Second-Floor Suite, R$350
Rua Francisco Sá 17
T 3222 8800
www.portinaridesignhotel.
com.br

026 Caesar Park
Room rates:
double, R$812;
Deluxe Room, R$972;
Junior Suite, R$1,429
Avenida Vieira Souto 460
T 2525 2525
www.caesarpark-rio.com

028 Brava Hotel
Room rates:
double, R$360–R$400
Rua 17, Lote 14, Quadra O
Praia Brava, Armação dos
Búzios
T 22 2623 5943
www.buziosonline.com.br/
bravahotel

24 HOURS

034 Café d'Hôtel
Avenida Delfim Moreira 696
T 2172 1100
www.marinaallsuites.com.br

035 Olympe
Rua Custódio Serrão 62
T 2539 4542
www.claudetroisgros.com.br

036 Jardim Botânico
Rua Jardim Botânico 1008
T 3874 1808
www.jbrj.gov.br

037 Guimas
Rua José Roberto Macedo
Soares 5
T 2259 7996

039 Garota de Ipanema
Rua Vinícius de Moraes 134
T 2522 0340

URBAN LIFE

**041 Espaço Cultural
Maurice Valansi**
Rua Martins Ferreira 48
T 2527 4044

042 Forneria Rio
Rua Aníbal de
Mendonça 112
T 2540 8045

044 Rio Scenarium
Rua do Lavradio 20
(nr Praca Tiradentes)
T 3147 9005
www.rioscenarium.com.br

045 Juice Co
Avenida General
San Martin 889
T 2294 0048

046 Academia da Cachaça
Rua Conde Bernadotte 26
T 2239 1542
www.academiadacachaca.
com.br

047 Estrela da Lapa
Avenida Mem de Sá 69
T 2507 6686
www.estreladalapa.
com.br

**048 Bar Luiz
Beach Kiosk**
Rua da Carioca 39
T 2262 6900
www.barluiz.com.br

050 Mil Frutas
Rua Garcia d'Ávila 134A
T 2521 1384
www.milfrutas.com.br

051 Devassa
Avenida General
San Martin 1241
T 2540 6087
www.devassa.com.br

052 Zuka
Rua Dias Ferreira 233
T 3205 7154

053 Confeitaria Colombo
Rua Gonçalves Dias 32
T 2232 2300
www.confeitariacolombo.
com.br

054 Sushi Leblon
Rua Dias Ferreira 256
T 2512 7830

056 Caroline Café
Rua JJ Seabra 10
T 2540 0705

057 Garcia e Rodrigues
Avenida Ataúlfo
de Paiva 1251
T 3206 4120
www.garciaerodrigues.
com.br

058 Carioca da Gema
Avenida Mem de Sá 79
T 2221 0043
www.barcariocadagema.
com.br

059 Bar d'Hotel
Marina All Suites Hotel,
Avenida Delfim Moreira 696
T 2540 4990

060 00
Planetário de Gávea,
Avenida Padre Leonel
França 240
T 2540 8041
www.00site.com.br

062 Clube Chocolate
Shopping Fashion Mall,
Estrada de Gávea 899
T 3322 3733
www.clubechocolate.com

062 Lulu
Rua Visconde de Carandaí 2
T 2294 7830

ARCHITOUR

065 Museu de Arte Contemporânea
Mirante da Boa Viagem,
Niterói
T 2620 2400

069 Sambódromo
Rua Marquês de Sapucaí

072 Palácio Gustavo Capanema
Rua da Imprensa 16

075 Petrobrás Building
Rua Lélio Gama 65

076 Museu de Arte Moderna (MAM)
Avenida Infante Dom Henrique 85
T 2240 4944
www.mamrio.com.br

077 Catédral Metropolitana
Avenida República do Chile 245
T 2240 2669
www.catedral.com.br

078 Parque Guinle
Rua Gago Coutinho 66-68 and Rua Paulo César de Andrade 70 and 106

SHOPPING

080 Isabela Capeto
Rua Dias Ferreira 45
T 2540 5232
www.isabelacapeto.com.br

080 Letras & Expressões
Avenida Ataúlfo de Paiva 1292
T 2511 5085
www.letraseexpressoes. com.br

080 Livraria da Travessa
Rua Visconde de Pirajá 572
T 3205 9002
www.livrariadatravessa. com.br

080 Modern Sound
Rua Barata Ribeiro 502
T 2548 5005
www.modernsound.com.br

081 Mercado Moderno
Rua do Lavradio 130
T 2508 6083
www.mercadomoderno brasil.com.br

082 Antonio Bernardo
Rua Garcia d'Ávila 121
T 2512 7204
www.antoniobernardo. com.br

083 Osklen
Rua Maria Quitéria 85
T 2227 2911
www.osklen.com

084 Atelier Ricardo Fasanello
Rua do Paraizo 42
T 2232 3164

084 Espasso
34-01 38 Avenue,
New York
T 00 1 718 472 0022
www.espasso.com

085 Loja Novo Desenho
Museu de Arte Moderna
Avenida Infante Dom Henrique 85
T 2524 2290

086 Maria Bonita
Rua Vinícius de Moraes 149
T 2523 4093

SPORTS AND SPAS

089 Maracanã Football Stadium
Rua Professor Eurico Rabela
T 2568 9962
www.suderj.rj.gov.br

092 Jóquei Clube Brasileiro
Rua Jardim Botânico 1003
T 2512 9988

094 Sítio do Lobo
Room rate:
double R$695
Ilha Grande
T 2227 4138
www.sitiodolobo.com.br

ESCAPES

097 DPNY Beach Hotel
Room rate:
double, R$170
Avenida José Pacheco do Nascimento 7668,
Praia do Curral,
Ilhabela, São Paulo
T 12 3894 2121
www.dpnybeach.com.br

WALLPAPER* CITY GUIDES

Editorial Director
Richard Cook

Art Director
Loran Stosskopf
City Editor
Nick Compton
Project Editor
Rachael Moloney
Series Editor
Jeroen Bergmans
**Executive
Managing Editor**
Jessica Firmin

Chief Designer
Ben Blossom
Designers
Sara Martin
Ingvild Sandal
Map Illustrator
Russell Bell

Photography Editor
James Reid
Photography Assistant
Jasmine Labeau

Chief Sub-Editor
Lizzie Stoodley
Sub-Editor
Clive Morris

Editorial Assistants
Felicity Cloake
Olivia Salazar-Winspear

**Wallpaper* Group
Editor-in-Chief**
Jeremy Langmead
Creative Director
Tony Chambers
Publishing Director
Fiona Dent

Thanks to
Paul Barnes
Emma Blau
Andrea Fasanello
Christopher Lands
David McKendrick
Claudia Perin
Meirion Pritchard

PHAIDON

Phaidon Press Limited
Regent's Wharf
All Saints Street
London N1 9PA

Phaidon Press Inc
180 Varick Street
New York, NY 10014

www.phaidon.com

First published 2006
© 2006 Phaidon Press
Limited

ISBN 0 7148 4694 5

A CIP Catalogue record for
this book is available from
the British Library.

All prices are correct at
time of going to press,
but are subject to change.

Printed in China

PHOTOGRAPHERS

Yann Arthus-Bertrand, Corbis
Maracaña Football Stadium, pp090-091

Christopher Griffith
Rio de Janeiro, City View, inside front cover
Sugar Loaf, pp010-011
Second World War Memorial, p012
Cristo Redentor, p013
Espaço Cultural Maurice Valansi, p041
Rio Scenarium, p044
Juice Co, p045
Zuka, p052
Confeitaria Colombo, p053
Insider's Guide, p063
Museu de Arte Contemporânea, p065
Sambódromo, pp068-071
Palácio Gustavo Capanema, pp072-073
Petrobrás Building, pp074-075
Museu de Arte Moderna, p076
Catédral Metropolitana, p077
Mercado Moderno, p081
Osklen, p083
Atelier Ricardo Fasanello, p084
Loja Novo Desenho, p085
Maracaña Football Stadium, p089
Joqúei Clube, p092

Mario Grisolli
Copacabana Promenade, pp014-015
Leblon Beach, p033
Café d'Hôtel, p034
Lagoa Rodrigo de Freitas, p035
Jardim Botânico, p036
Guimas, p037
Ipanema Beach, p038
Garota de Ipanema, p039
Forneria Rio, pp042-043
Academia da Cachaça, p046
Estrela da Lapa, p047
Bar Luiz Beach Kiosk, pp048-049
Mil Frutas, p050
Devassa, p051
Sushi Leblon, pp054-055
Caroline Café, p056
Garcia e Rodrigues, p057
Carioca da Gema, p058
Bar d'Hôtel, p059
00, pp060-061
Antonio Bernardo, p082
Maria Bonita, pp086-087
Floresta da Tijuca, p093

David Hughes
Ilhabela, pp097-099

Nelson Kon
Parque Guinle, pp078-079

Joerg Schoener, Artur
Museu de Arte Contemporânea, pp066-067
Brasília, pp100-103

RIO DE JANEIRO
A COLOUR-CODED GUIDE TO THE CITY'S HOT 'HOODS

LEBLON
While the rest of the city is hot and hectic, Rio's smartest burg is cool and calm

CENTRO
Rio's historic downtown is a steamy mix of modernism and old colonial

LAGOA
A stunning lagoon, ringed by swanky apartments and lively restaurants

IPANEMA
The girls here are as beautiful as the song and legend suggest. Nice beach, too

COPACABANA
The curved beach is a beauty, but Copacabana is overdue a clean-up

SANTA TERESA
Elegantly decayed mansion houses and boho locals sitting high above the city

LAPA
Rio's new party central. This is where the samba sways, but not gently

For a full description of each neighbourhood,
including the places you really must not miss, see the Introduction